THE CIVIL WAR
EARLY BATTLES

BY JIM OLLHOFF

VISIT US AT
WWW.ABDOPUBLISHING.COM

Published by ABDO Publishing Company, PO Box 398166, Minneapolis, MN 55439. Copyright ©2012 by Abdo Consulting Group, Inc. International copyrights reserved in all countries. No part of this book may be reproduced in any form without written permission from the publisher. ABDO & Daughters™ is a trademark and logo of ABDO Publishing Company.

Printed in the United States of America, North Mankato, Minnesota.
112011
012012

Editor: John Hamilton
Graphic Design: John Hamilton
Cover Design: Neil Klinepier
Cover Photo: Getty Images
Interior Photos and Illustrations: Corbis, p. 7, 7 (inset), 22-23; DigitalStock, p. 3, 10, 11, 13, 18-19, 21, 26-27, 28; Getty Images, p. 16, 18, 19, 25, 26, 29; iStockphoto, p. 4-5; John Hamilton, p. 9, 14-15, 17, 24, 27; Hal Jespersen, www.posix.com/cw, p. 24, 27; Library of Congress, p. 6; National Archives, p. 20; ThinkStock, p. 8-9.

ABDO Booklinks
To learn more about the Civil War, visit ABDO Publishing Company online. Web sites about the Civil War are featured on our Book Links pages. These links are routinely monitored and updated to provide the most current information available. Web site: www.abdopublishing.com

Library of Congress Cataloging-in-Publication Data

Ollhoff, Jim, 1959-
  The Civil War : early battles / Jim Ollhoff.
     p. cm. -- (The Civil War)
  Includes index.
  ISBN 978-1-61783-273-4
  1. United States--History--Civil War, 1861-1865--Campaigns--Juvenile literature. I. Title.
  E470.O45 2012
  973.7'31--dc23
                    2011038457

CONTENTS

Union soldiers from New York.

THE ROAD TO WAR

In December 1860, South Carolina became the first state to secede from the Union. Mississippi, Florida, Alabama, Georgia, Louisiana, and Texas soon followed. Later, Virginia, Arkansas, Tennessee, and North Carolina also seceded. These states banded together to form the Confederate States of America.

Abraham Lincoln had been elected in November 1860, but his presidency didn't begin until March 1861. James Buchanan was the president when the Southern states began to secede from the Union, but he did little to stop them.

The Confederacy created a government in February 1861, with its capital in Richmond, Virginia. Jefferson Davis was named president.

The Southern states began to seize federal property—forts, ammunition supply depots, harbor ports, even post offices. President James Buchanan still did nothing.

In March 1861, Abraham Lincoln became president. He had no immediate plans to end slavery in the South, but he would not accept the secession of the Southern states. Both Abraham Lincoln and Jefferson Davis were still hoping to resolve the situation peacefully, but the chances of that seemed grim. Both Lincoln and Davis asked for volunteers to strengthen their armies.

THE SIEGE OF FORT SUMTER

Before the war started, Union troops were stationed in Charleston, South Carolina. When South Carolina seceded from the Union in December 1860, Union troops needed to protect themselves. They retreated to a fort in Charleston Harbor called Fort Sumter.

The Confederacy didn't like Union troops occupying Fort Sumter. The Confederates believed the fort was their property. They demanded that the Union troops at Fort Sumter surrender. The Union troops refused. Tensions rose.

Finally, on April 12, 1861, Confederate troops began firing cannons at the walls of Fort Sumter. Union troops returned fire. After 34 hours of shelling, neither side did much damage. Union troops were low on food and ammunition, and so they raised the white flag of surrender. The first shots had been fired, but there were no combat deaths. Still, tensions had boiled over. The Civil War had begun.

The Confederate flag flying above captured Fort Sumter.

Confederate forces firing on Fort Sumter in Charleston Harbor, South Carolina.

7

THE CIVIL WAR BEGINS

The victory at Fort Sumter raised the morale of the Southern states. They were determined not to be controlled by the North. However, the South had several weaknesses. They didn't have an army. They pulled together a few thousand Federal soldiers who had sympathies for the South. They got volunteers, but they were farmers, merchants, and plantation owners who had little war training. The South had no navy ships, but managed to confiscate cannons.

The South also had fewer people than the North. The South only had about nine million people. Four million were slaves. Twenty-one million people lived in Northern states. The North had more railroads, more factories, and more businesses that made guns.

The South had one big advantage. It's easier to defend your homeland than it is to attack somewhere else. Southern soldiers were very familiar with their land. They needed to simply dig in and wait for an attack.

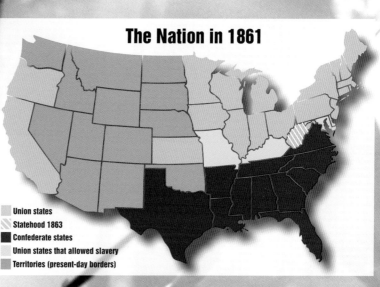

The Nation in 1861

Union states
Statehood 1863
Confederate states
Union states that allowed slavery
Territories (present-day borders)

Men dressed as Union and Confederate Civil War soldiers reenact a battle scene.

Union forces would have to travel long distances. They would have to find ways to bring food to feed their huge armies. They also had to figure out how to transport ammunition and supplies over long distances.

One unknown factor was Europe. England and France got most of their cotton from the Southern states. How badly did Europe need Southern cotton? The Confederacy hoped that England and France would send their massive armies to aid the South.

No army can exist without good military leadership. Union forces only had a few officers who had served in combat. Lincoln offered the command of the Union armies to the best strategist he had: Robert E. Lee. But Lee couldn't fight against his native Virginia, even though he disagreed with the idea of secession. He was loyal to

Confederate General Robert E. Lee was asked by President Lincoln to lead the Union army, but the brilliant commander decided instead to fight for his home state of Virginia.

his home state, and so he went to serve the South. Lee was a brilliant general. He gave the Southern armies a huge advantage in the early fighting of the war.

Opposite page: The Union 96th Pennsylvania infantry regiment in camp in 1861, training with rifles. One of the biggest challenges for the Union army was transporting its soldiers and equipment over long distances.

Soldiers of the Civil War

WHY DID MEN VOLUNTEER?

President Abraham Lincoln, leader of the Union, and President Jefferson Davis, leader of the Confederacy, both called for men to volunteer to fight. During the Civil War, soldiers died by the thousands. Bullets tore away body parts. There were no antibiotics and few available pain-killing medications. Amputation with a hacksaw was the likely end to a leg or arm wound. Twice as many soldiers died of infection and disease as from combat wounds. Men traveled far from their homes and families, and were asked to fight in the worst conditions imaginable. So why did they volunteer?

Soldiers volunteered for the same reasons they volunteer for military duty today. They loved their country. They were promised a good salary and food to eat. Many who had never been more than a few miles from home were excited about traveling to far-away places. Many put on their uniform and realized it was the best suit of clothes they'd ever owned.

Some men joined to fight slavery. Others joined to keep the union of states together. But no one realized that the war would be so long, so horrible, and so bloody. Most people thought the war would be over in a few weeks or months.

A group of soldiers waits to be called up for battle.

13

FIRST BATTLE OF BULL RUN

The leadership of the North thought stopping the Southern rebellion would be quick and easy. President Lincoln called for army volunteers, but said they would be needed only for three months. Many people thought a single battle victory would end the war.

Several small fights broke out across the country, but the first big battle of the Civil War was at the Bull Run Creek in northern Virginia. Union forces called it the Battle of Bull Run. Confederate forces called it the Battle of Manassas, since it was near the town of Manassas Junction, Virginia. Later, this battle became known as the *First Battle of Bull Run*. A second battle was fought in the same place a year later.

In July 1861, about 38,000 Union troops, commanded by General Irvin McDowell, marched south toward Richmond, Virginia, the Confederate capital. Just weeks earlier, these soldiers had been farmers and merchants. They were largely untrained, and were rushed into battle.

Artillery (background) fires on the enemy as Union soldiers advance on Confederate positions in a reenactment of the First Battle of Bull Run.

Confederate infantry advance on Union lines during a reenactment of the Civil War's First Battle of Bull Run, near Manassas, Virginia.

The Confederate forces in Virginia, about 22,000 men under the command of General Pierre Beauregard, marched to meet the Union army. The two sides met at Bull Run Creek in northern Virginia.

People from Washington, D.C., had come out to the scene to watch the Union win the war. Some people brought their families and food for a picnic. No one imagined that this battle, or the war itself, would be so long and terrible.

On July 21, 1861, the battle began. Union forces began shelling Confederate positions with their cannons. But the Union army had an overly complicated battle plan that required complex troop movements. Union forces, untrained and unable to mount a coordinated attack, were driven back by Confederate troops.

During the battle, Confederate General Thomas Jackson bravely held a hill from the approaching

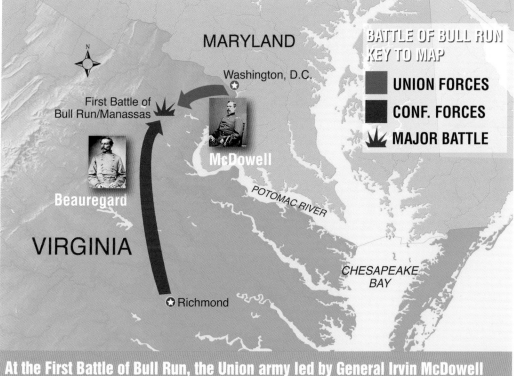

MARYLAND

Washington, D.C.

First Battle of
Bull Run/Manassas

McDowell

Beauregard

POTOMAC RIVER

VIRGINIA

CHESAPEAKE
BAY

Richmond

N

At the First Battle of Bull Run, the Union army led by General Irvin McDowell was defeated by Confederate forces led by General Pierre Beauregard.

Union forces. Another officer declared, "There is Jackson standing like a stone wall!" After that, General Jackson became known as "Stonewall" Jackson. He was a gifted military strategist, and became one of General Robert E. Lee's most trusted battlefield generals.

Lines and positions shifted throughout the day. Finally, fresh Confederate reinforcements arrived by railroad to the battlefield. This caused a panic in the untrained Union troops, and they fell back and ran. The retreating Union forces became entangled with the fleeing picnickers. The Union army had collapsed into chaos, but the rebel army was too tired to give chase.

The Union lost 2,900 soldiers that day to death, wounds, or desertion. The Confederates lost about 2,000 men. The level of violence shocked each side. Predictions of a short, easy war faced an ugly reality: the Civil War would be long and bloody.

THE ANACONDA PLAN

After the Union defeat at Bull Run, President Abraham Lincoln was certain that a longer war was ahead. The president called together his generals to form new strategies.

President Abraham Lincoln (left) and General Winfield Scott (left, standing) at a council of war discussing Union plans.

One of Lincoln's oldest military leaders, General Winfield Scott, proposed a plan to defeat the South. It was nicknamed the Anaconda Plan, after the South American snake that wraps around its prey and squeezes the life out of it.

Scott's plan had three major parts: 1) March south and take Richmond, Virginia, the Confederate capital. 2) Control the Mississippi River, and capture the towns bordering the river. 3) Take the Union navy and blockade Confederate ports, preventing supplies from entering the Confederacy and stopping the South from exporting cotton.

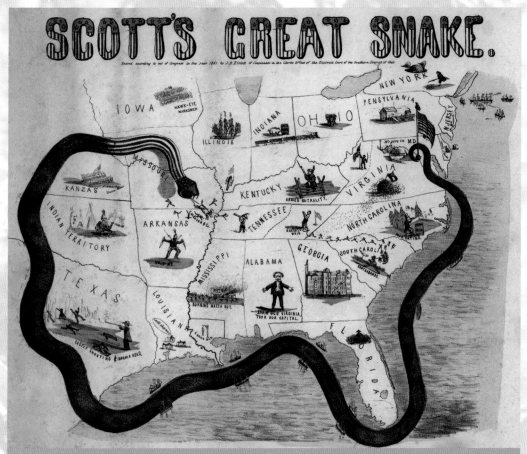

SCOTT'S GREAT SNAKE.

An 1861 cartoon illustrating General Winfield Scott's plan to encircle and crush the Confederacy by preventing the export and import of supplies.

Newspapers mocked the Anaconda Plan. They said it was too cautious. But Lincoln, who realized that the war would not be over anytime soon, saw the plan's wisdom and put it into effect. However, the Union was not ready for a long, complicated war. Its army was small, and new recruits were undisciplined and untrained. The navy had only a few ships that could work as blockade vessels, and the South had almost 200 ports that needed to be blockaded. The Union immediately began building and purchasing as many ships as possible to carry out the Anaconda Plan.

President Lincoln appointed General George McClellan to be in charge of training new army recruits. McClellan was a great organizer and trainer of new soldiers. However, as a battlefield general, he repeatedly bungled his campaigns.

Union General George McClellan

Lincoln ordered McClellan to take his army south toward Richmond, Virginia, but McClellan seemed afraid to attack the enemy. He always wanted to wait for more reinforcements, and sometimes simply ignored Lincoln's orders.

The North was unprepared for war, but conditions were worse in the South. President Jefferson Davis called for volunteers, but there was little money to offer them pay. Many of the soldiers had to use rifles left over from previous wars because the South lacked gun-manufacturing factories.

Another disadvantage for the South was that it had begun with the idea that each state, not the central government, was the highest authority. People in the South were suspicious of any action by Jefferson Davis's government, even when the president called for volunteers to defend the Confederacy.

Knowing of the South's disadvantages, President Lincoln hoped that the controversial Anaconda Plan would work. Eventually, the strategy was proven effective. The Anaconda Plan put a chokehold on the South. But in the meantime, there were four long years of battles to be fought.

Opposite page: D.W.C. Arnold, a private in the Union army. The Union had more troops than the Confederacy, but both sides needed training to be ready for battle.

21

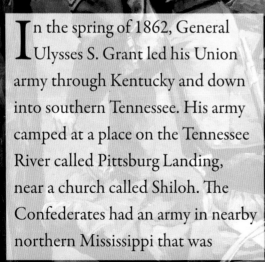

April 1862

THE BATTLE OF SHILOH

In the spring of 1862, General Ulysses S. Grant led his Union army through Kentucky and down into southern Tennessee. His army camped at a place on the Tennessee River called Pittsburg Landing, near a church called Shiloh. The Confederates had an army in nearby northern Mississippi that was protecting an important railroad junction.

Grant's Union army was full of new soldiers. They hadn't built up any defenses around their encampment. They hadn't done enough exploring to see if any Confederate armies were nearby. On Sunday morning, April 6, while

Plenty of Fighting Today by artist Keith Rocco. Union troops of the 9th Illinois at the Battle of Shiloh.

many Union soldiers were still asleep, thousands of Confederate soldiers crashed through the forest toward the camp.

The Confederate army tried to maintain too big a front line. Some soldiers were too far ahead and some were too far back. Officers couldn't give orders because they couldn't find their men in the heavily wooded area.

The Union soldiers were in total chaos, some fleeing and others shooting into the woods. The Battle of Shiloh quickly became two mobs of uncoordinated people shooting at each other.

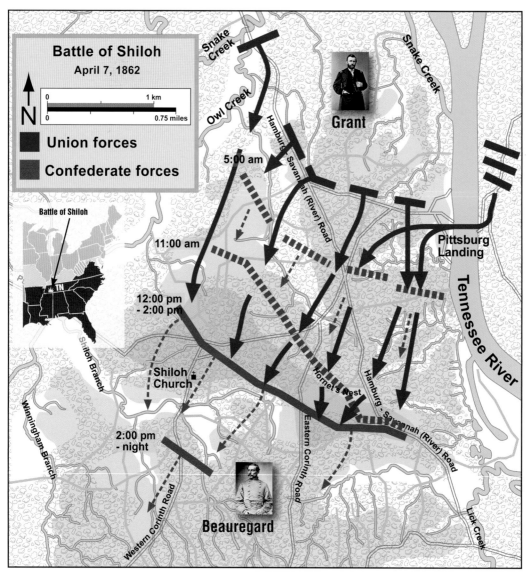

Battle of Shiloh
April 7, 1862

N

0 — 1 km
0 — 0.75 miles

Union forces
Confederate forces

Battle of Shiloh

TN

Snake Creek

Owl Creek

Hamburg - Savannah (River) Road

Grant

Snake Creek

Pittsburg Landing

Tennessee River

5:00 am

11:00 am

12:00 pm - 2:00 pm

Shiloh Branch

Winningham Branch

Shiloh Church

2:00 pm - night

Hornet's Nest

Eastern Corinth Road

Hamburg - Savannah (River) Road

Western Corinth Road

Beauregard

Lick Creek

Union General Grant stood among his men, trying to muster enough of a force to counterattack. He called for reinforcements from a nearby army. Confederate General Albert Sidney Johnston had Grant's army in a dangerous situation, and knew he had to act quickly. Although his troops were scattered, he gathered enough men to charge the Union line. Johnston led his troops from the front, and he was shot and killed. The Union forces fell back to a natural defensive position nicknamed the "Hornet's Nest." Confederate forces tried to

General Ulysses Grant (right, on horseback) directs his Union troops to victory against the Confederates at the Battle of Shiloh.

take the position, but were held back. This gave the Union precious time for reinforcements to arrive.

Confederate General Beauregard was miles away from the front lines, and wasn't aware of what was going on. He told his Confederate forces to stop and rest. He mistakenly believed that the Union army was all but destroyed, and that the Confederate army could finish up the battle the next day. This gave Union reinforcements the time they needed to get organized.

On the morning of April 7, 1862, Confederate forces suddenly realized they were facing a much bigger army than the previous day. The Union troops advanced, pushing the Confederate forces back. With both armies exhausted and running out of ammunition, each side finally fled the battlefield.

The Union won the Battle of Shiloh, but the aftermath was horrific. About one-fourth of the soldiers died. Observers said that the battlefield was so thick with bodies that a person could walk across the area without ever stepping on the ground. More than 13,000 Union soldiers and 10,000 Confederate soldiers were dead, captured, or wounded.

September 1862

THE BATTLE OF ANTIETAM

Confederate General Robert E. Lee needed to take pressure off the constant attacks to his army. He thought that if he took his army to the North, then the Union forces might become too spread out. So he took his army northward toward Pennsylvania.

Union General McClellan pursued Lee. McClellan's Union army was twice the size of Lee's army, but McClellan continued to be too cautious a commander. McClellan even found a copy of Lee's battle plans, but he was still afraid to attack. Many historians believe that had McClellan attacked Lee, he would have won the battle, and the Civil War would have been over early.

The armies finally met at the small town of Sharpsburg, Maryland, near Antietam Creek. On September 17, 1862, they fought the Battle of Antietam (called the Battle of Sharpsburg in the South). It was the first major

The Battle of Antietam

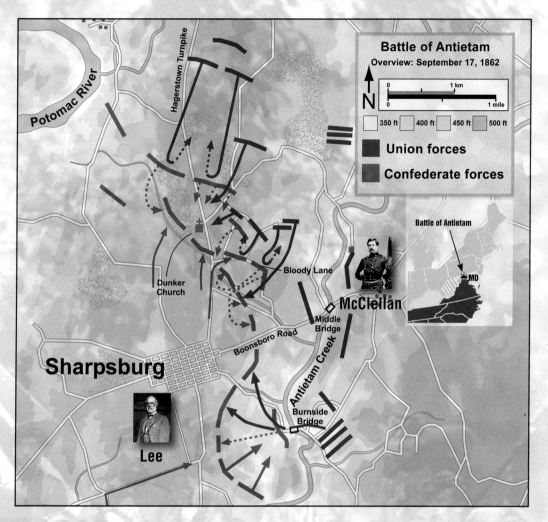

Battle of Antietam
Overview: September 17, 1862

0   1 km
0   1 mile

350 ft   400 ft   450 ft   500 ft

Union forces

Confederate forces

Battle of Antietam

MD

Potomac River

Hagerstown Turnpike

Dunker Church

Bloody Lane

McClellan

Middle Bridge

Boonsboro Road

Antietam Creek

Sharpsburg

Burnside Bridge

Lee

conflict to be fought in Northern territory.

A bloody battle raged, but Union General McClellan still refused to commit enough troops to the fighting. This gave Lee the time to stop the Union's half-hearted attacks. Lee soon realized he was vastly outnumbered. He and his army retreated back to Virginia.

McClellan refused to give chase. Although the battle was a Union victory, McClellan missed a chance to destroy the Confederate army.

The Battle of Antietam was the bloodiest one-day battle of the Civil War. The Confederates lost more than 10,000 men to death or wounds. The Union lost more than 12,000 men.

The Emancipation Proclamation
AT THE END OF 1862

By the end of 1862, hundreds of battles had been fought throughout many states. Overall, the Union was having difficulty. It was hobbled by ineffective or incompetent generals.

On the other hand, Confederate General Robert E. Lee was proving to be a brilliant strategist. He seemed to know how his adversaries were moving and what they were thinking. He always seemed to be one step ahead of the Union armies.

Even though the South won many of the early Civil War battles, it had many problems. There weren't enough Confederate soldiers, and there was too little money. The Union, on the other hand, seemed to have an endless supply of soldiers, weapons, and ammunition.

Shortly after the Battle of Antietam, President Lincoln revealed a stunning game-changer. His Emancipation Proclamation said that by January 1, 1863, slaves in areas of rebellion would be officially declared free. It was a declaration for the dignity of people everywhere. Although he couldn't actually set the Southern slaves free until after a Union victory, Lincoln's executive order changed the nature of the Civil War. It was now about preserving the union *and* freedom from slavery. The Emancipation Proclamation increased support for the Union cause.

President Abraham Lincoln (left) talks with General George McClellan in the general's headquarters tent after the Battle of Antietam. Lincoln was unhappy that McClellan did not pursue the Confederate forces after the Union victory.

7948

GLOSSARY

ANACONDA PLAN

The Union's plan to squeeze the South, by blockading ports, sending an army toward Richmond, and seizing control of the Mississippi River and nearby cities.

BLOCKADE

To prevent ships from entering or leaving a port.

CIVIL WAR

A war where two parts of the same nation fight against each other. The American Civil War was fought between Northern and Southern states from 1861–1865. The Southern states were for slavery. They wanted to start their own country. Northern states fought against slavery and a division of the country.

CONFEDERACY

The Southern states of Alabama, Arkansas, Florida, Georgia, Louisiana, Mississippi, North Carolina, South Carolina, Tennessee, Texas, and Virginia. These states wanted to keep slavery legal. They broke away from the United States during the Civil War and formed their own country known as the Confederate States of America, or the Confederacy. The Confederacy ended in 1865 when the war ended and the 11 Confederate states rejoined the United States.

CONFISCATE

To take something away, sometimes by force, especially by law enforcement or the military. At the beginning of the Civil War, the Confederacy confiscated military equipment such as cannons left by the Union army.

EMANCIPATION PROCLAMATION

On September 22, 1862, President Abraham Lincoln announced that slaves in all states still in rebellion against the United States would be set free. His executive order took effect on January 1, 1863. The word emancipation means to be set free. For many African Americans, emancipation after the Civil War meant freedom from slavery.

EXECUTIVE ORDER

An order issued by the president of the United States, as the head of the Executive Branch of the U.S. government. Executive orders are like laws that don't go through the usual process of first being passed by Congress.

PLANTATION

A large farm where crops such as tobacco, sugar cane, and cotton are grown. Workers usually live right on the property. Early plantation owners in North America used cheap slave labor to make their operations more profitable.

SECEDE

To withdraw membership in a union or alliance.

UNION

The Northern states united against the Confederacy. "Union" also refers to all of the states of the United States. President Lincoln wanted to preserve the Union, keeping the Northern and Southern states together.

INDEX